Poetic Path

Thoughts on Freedom and Life

Ella Cassa

BookLeaf Publishing
India | USA | UK

Made with ❤ on the BookLeaf Publishing Platform
www.bookleafpub.in
www.bookleafpub.com

Dedication

To you, the bold dreamer, the unyielding spirit, the one brave enough to defy boundaries and shape a life that is unmistakably your own.

This collection is dedicated to the fearless hearts who refuse to be confined by conventions or subdued by the weight of others' expectations. It's for those who venture into the unknown, even when the comfort of the familiar whispers for their return, and for those who seek and celebrate the untamed, honest beauty of living authentically.

May these words kindle the quiet flame of your inner wisdom and inspire you to honour the rhythm of your own heartbeat. With every step you take toward your truth, you are crafting a masterpiece of resilience, courage, and self-expression, claiming a life that is as unique and extraordinary as your spirit.

Here's to your courage, your strength, and the breathtaking vision of a path only you can carve. Keep moving forward, keep growing, and never stop creating a world that reflects the unparalleled power of who you truly are.

Preface

Poetry has a way of transforming a personal thought into something universal. It bridges the gap between individual experience and shared understanding, inviting us to feel, reflect, and connect. *Poetic Path: Thoughts on Freedom and Life* is more than just a collection of verses; it is a map of my soul etched through moments of raw honesty, growth, and discovery.

Inspired by confessional poetry, these verses chart my journey, capturing profound moments of transformation and self-discovery. Writing them was not just an act of expression but a deeply fulfilling process, allowing me to embrace the truths that have shaped me. I hope these words will resonate with your story, celebrating the shared threads defining the beauty of life's journeys.

May these verses remind you of the strength in owning your voice, the freedom in living your truth, and the joy that blossoms when we connect through our shared stories. Thank you for joining me on this poetic path.

Acknowledgements

To Aryan Saha, my honourable friend, and to everyone who has walked beside me, your presence has left an indelible mark on these pages. To all who have shared brief moments or lasting memories, your kindness, lessons, and even the smallest gestures have shaped me as both a person and a writer. This collection carries the whispers of our shared experiences and traces of how they guided my path.

To those who held faith in me when I couldn't find it within myself, you are the quiet heroes of my story. Your belief, often stronger than mine, helped me move forward when the road felt steep and uncertain. I also owe a quiet thanks to myself for finding the strength to listen to my heart, even when doubt clouded my way. Thank you for refusing to give up and believing that light can still be found when you trust your chosen path.

I owe my deepest gratitude to all of you. Your company, hope, and steadfast presence have breathed life into this work. This book exists because of you and because I have learned, through all of it, that none of us truly walks this path alone.

1. Whispers of the Way

A single word, a whispered start,
A gentle pull within the heart.
Through verses carved and dreams unspun,
A world of wonder has begun.

Each step we take, a story grows,
Through highs and lows, the rhythm flows.
Walk this path, both bright and true,
And find the poet inside you.

2. The Weight of Arrival

To come to this world,
in a place, in a family,
chosen or not.
A quiet mystery unfolds.

Born under the sun or the shadow,
where flowers bloom, or thorns take hold.
You are thrust into life,
to live, to strive, to grow.

A contradiction beats in every breath,
a gift, a burden, a winding road.
Hardship may whisper,
"Stay small, stay low."
Comfort may hum,
"Rest easy, don't go."

But YOU,
yes, you, hold the pen,
to write beyond
a past's script.

Circumstance is loud,
but you are louder still.

3. Paper Boats of Hope

In childhood's grip, we wander lost,
Destiny's dice. We pay the cost.

With dreams like fragile paper boats,
We hope for hands that guide and float.

For in their care, our futures thrive,
And only then, we learn to strive.

4. Roots of Tomorrow

When you are a child,
the world decides for you.
At the mercy of hands unknown,
you wait, hope, and trust.

Destiny rolls its silent dice,
Luck leans in with fickle breath.
And if no kind soul holds you close,
you learn, you bend and survive.

A soothing voice, a steady hand,
A shield from winds both harsh and cold.
Without their care, the light may fade,
Leaving young hearts to face the cold.

Each child is born with endless worlds,
a future waiting to unfold.
What they create, we'll only know,
if given love, if made whole.

5. Melody of My Choosing

A dance of rules, a game to play,
A script to follow, come what may.
But no, my friend, I step away,
To carve a tune my heart can play.

I abstain amidst the critical glare,
Their eyes like mirrors, unaware.
"Not free will," they'd try to claim,
Yet beauty thrives in chaos' name.

Faith hums steadily, a looped refrain,
A tune well-worn, both sweet and plain.
The concert's done, the echoes fade,
Yet I seek notes that won't betray.

In the Symphony of Faith, I stray,
Where shadows shift and truths delay.
Each day, I write a daring verse,
A melody to break the universe.

Seeking paths, both wild and clear,
Crafting art against the fear.
Guided by love, respect as guide,
A compass strong, my course untied

6. Dreams in Bloom

A scatter of stardust softly gleams,
Cradling whispers, shaping dreams.
Through the hush, worlds take flight,
A fire blazes in the silent night.

I drift where thought and shadow meet,
On silky threads, where hearts retreat.
A fragile pearl, aglow with might,
Sows a spark in the cradle of night.

Threads unseen, I weave with care,
A living map to the dreams we dare.
Each spark a wish, a cosmic spree,
Forever twined with what could be.

7. Silent Echoes

Emotions unseen,
Everything's fine.
Silent signals call,
But there's no time.

Always polished, always kind,
A perfect act, a script assigned.
Cinderella's gown hides the truth,
Neglect becomes the tale of youth.

Alone, adrift in my own space,
Lost within a crowded place.
Yearning faintly for a spark,
A banquet was served with no remark.

Too small, too young to be heard,
My voice is trapped, just a whispered word.
Yet still I stand, I won't subside,
Writing the truth I hold inside.

8. Unbreakable Soul

Beneath your shadow, I once bent low,
But every day, my strength will grow.

You shift the tides; you grasp control,
Yet I restore, piece by piece, my soul.

Enjoy this reign while you hold it near,
For I'll rise stronger; the truth is clear.

No power stays; like leaves, will fall,
Even a spark can outshine it all.

9. Threads of Us

Born into bonds we did not choose,
Woven in textures we cannot lose.
Father's silence, steady and strong,
A presence that held me all along.

Mother's care, both fierce and kind,
A thread of love that will not unwind.
Brother's laugh, a fading tune,
Yet it lingers beneath the moon.

Sister's hand, in mine once tight,
Now, a whisper in the quiet night.
Strangers crossed my path unseen,
Left their marks in moments between.

A kind word here, a glance that stayed,
Threads of chance that time can't fade.
And my homeland's fields, its skies of blue,
Shaped the roots of all I knew.

Its winds still carry me back each day,
Though life may pull me far away.
Hands that broke, yet reached again,
Bound by threads that never end.

10. Mirror of myself

Nice to meet you. A reflection of my soul.
In this mirror, as a whole.
I stand waiting, embracing all.

Memories flicker in these eyes,
both the joy and the trials,
each facet of my life,
mirrored back, a striking sight.

Imperfections, yes, they're clear,
Yet, they mark paths I hold dear.
My strengths shine just as bright,
In this self-reflective light.

Through this looking glass, I behold,
An ever-evolving version of myself, bold.
I welcome every part of the light, the dark.

On this path, uniquely mine,
reflecting the essence of my time.
With an open heart, I walk along a poetic path,
crafting my unique style,
Reflecting myself through verse and rhyme,
Choosing a journey truly mine.

11. On Your Watching

You saw me stumble,
Lost and small.
Your gaze was heavy,
But you decide to pass it all

A nod, a shrug,
Then you turned away.
I begged for rescue,
You stayed at bay.

A hero? A ghost?
I'll never know.
You lit no path,
But made me grow.

Your silence lingered,
It burned like flame.
Yet here I stand,
On my own two feet.

12. An Open Truth

I'm not here to judge,
To stir the stillness,
Dust off the silence,
And see what lingers.

Your love felt clear,
But the path was rough.
I sought light,
Yet trust was tough.

Can we share fears,
Lay them bare?
Two voices meeting,
Truth in the air.

13. Defying The Current

I walk my path, though winds may crash,
With every step, I shape and clash.
Finding hearts, both kind and wild,
Against the dark, my spirit smiled—
In defiance, I find freedom's core.

A long road behind, half-life now gone,
Three lands, an ocean between us drawn.
Rules in sore ink of what should be,
Choices loom; time watches me.

Lost in shadows, I seek my way,
A journey unfolds, day by day.
Meeting my voice, to rise, to glow,
Piece by piece, my soul will grow.

The tide may pull, the waves may rise,
Yet I stand firm beneath the skies.
Through storms and doubt, I will abide,
For I am me—**against the tide.**

14. Chosen Family

We met by luck, a happy chance,
No shared roots, but a shared dance.

Through twists and turns, laughter and tears,
You've been my stone across the years.
No need for words, you just know,
Through every high and every low.

You see my scars, the mess, the flaws,
And love me still without a pause.
With you, it's comfort, it's bright, it's home,
Even when the world has me roam.

Chosen family, tried and true,
Life's just better with friends like you.

15. Rising Above

The road was rough, the skies were grey,
But I stayed strong and found my way.

Through every fall, I rose once more,
A spark within, my lasting core.

The nights were long, their voices loud,
Yet still, I stood, unbowed, unbowed.

Each scar I wear tells a story,
Of battles fought and courage bold.

Now here I stand, the darkness gone,
The sun is bright, and I move on.

16. Unspoken Friends

They do not speak in words we know,
Yet in their gaze, emotions show.
A wag, a bark, a gentle paw,
Their language vivid, without flaw.

Days they share, both short and long,
Their presence steady, quiet, strong.
No need for phrases, letters, lines,
Their love is pure, their bond divine.

Through joy, through loss, they softly stay,
They light the dark, they mend the fray.
Each step beside, their souls align,
Their hearts a gift, a sacred sign.

Though time may take their earthly form,
Their essence lingers, safe and warm.
Forever friends, their spirits true,
An endless love they give to you.

17. Voice of the Heart

Through the noise, a call unseen,
Quiet, steady, pure, serene.

When darkness looms and hope runs thin,
The heart ignites a spark within.

No need for maps, trust, just feel,
Its silent truth, constant and real.

A flame of courage, fierce and bright,
Guides the soul through endless night.

18. Silent Reflections

Beneath the glow, the quiet sings,
A stillness soft, where wisdom clings.
The echoes fade, the heart takes flight,
To find its truth in tranquil light.

A thought unknown begins to bloom,
Amid the hush, dissolving gloom.
No need for words, no need for cries,
The answers rest where silence lies.

Through gentle calm, the soul is free,
Its whispers shape what's meant to be.
The weight is gone, the peace remains,
A quiet strength in love's refrains.

19. Sleeping Dreams

Dreams may fade, but never die,
Softly stirring beneath the sky.
Quiet shadows of light once known,
They linger still, though time has grown.

Hidden deep, their glow remains,
A whispered hope in life's refrains.
Like dawn that warms the coldest night,
They wait to bloom in newfound light.

With gentle hands, their spark ignites,
A flame reborn from embered nights.
Dreams don't vanish, they only rest,
Guiding us toward what's next, what's best.

20. The Heart of Freedom

Freedom is air, a boundless sky,
A whisper of dreams where hopes can fly.
It's breaking chains, a step renewed,
The strength to choose, the courage to pursue.

For some, it's peace, a quiet land,
For others, the will to take a stand.
It's not one shape, but countless streams,
A life unbound, alive with dreams.

21. Poetic Voice

A blank page calls, a quiet spark,
A flame ignites within the dark.
Through every word, a world takes flight,
A map of thought, a trail of light.

Each stanza carved with tender hands,
A bridge that time itself withstands.
It speaks of love, of loss, of grace,
And weaves connections, space to space.

Through pain and joy, through night and day,
Poetry shapes what words can't say.
It binds us close, though far apart,
A common thread from heart to heart.

Each verse a seed, a voice set free,
A ripple in eternity.
Through written truth, we dare believe,
A legacy we all conceive.

www.ingramcontent.com/pod-product-compliance
Lightning Source LLC
Chambersburg PA
CBHW062110140826
49812CB00058B/1240